Brain Gain

How Brain-Computer Interfaces Are Changing the World

Taylor Royce

DEDICATION

To those with the audacity to envision a time when the limits of human potential are continuously redefined and enlarged. This book is devoted to the visionary individuals scientists, researchers, engineers, and dreamers whose unwavering quest for knowledge and creativity has advanced our understanding of a future in which the merging of human and machine intelligence holds extraordinary potential.

To those whose lives are irrevocably changed by the developments in Brain-Computer Interfaces, and to those who bravely and resolutely confront the challenges of neurological illnesses and impairments. The work that is shown in these pages is inspired by your courage and determination.

To the teachers and mentors who shape the minds and works of the upcoming generation of thinkers and artists by fostering in them a sense of ethical duty, curiosity, and a desire to change the world for the better.

Lastly, I hope this book will be a source of knowledge, motivation, and a call to action for all those who are interested in learning about and interacting with the cutting edge of human-machine interaction. I see a time when technology will further improve and elevate the human experience.

CONTENTS

ACKNOWLEDGMENTS

The result of many years of hard work, devotion, and cooperation is this book. Without the help, direction, and contributions of several people and organizations, it would not have been feasible.

First and foremost, I would like to sincerely thank the respected authorities and investigators in the field of Brain-Computer Interfaces (BCIs). This investigation has been anchored by your innovative work and thoughts, which served as the basis for this book. A special thank you to everyone who kindly answered my questions, gave their expertise, and provided insightful criticism.

I want to express my sincere gratitude to my mentors and colleagues, who have supported and encouraged me at every turn during this trip. Your suggestions, helpful critiques, and steadfast faith in this effort have been crucial in determining the course and caliber of the material.

The real-world experiences and practical ideas shared by the devoted professionals and practitioners in the fields of

BCI technology, medicine, and cognitive improvement have substantially enhanced this book. Your contributions have given the conversations on the opportunities and difficulties posed by BCIs a crucial point of view.

My sincere gratitude goes out to my family and friends for their tolerance, comprehension, and support. Your encouragement and strength have helped me to overcome the difficulties associated with writing and research.

To the editors and publishing team, I express my gratitude for your hard work and knowledge in making this book a reality. Your painstaking attention to detail and dedication to quality have been really helpful in enhancing and presenting the content in the most effective manner.

Finally, I thank the numerous people and institutions whose contributions in relevant domains have influenced and educated this book. You have made significant contributions to society, ethics, and technology that have given important perspective and insight.

I express my gratitude to all those who contributed to the creation of this book. Your combined efforts have enabled and meaningfully contributed to this investigation into

Brain-Computer Interfaces and its implications for human potential.

DISCLAIMER

The material in this book is not professional advice; rather, it is meant to be used for general informational purposes only. Although every effort has been taken to ensure that the content is accurate and complete, certain information may become outdated or may not fully reflect current developments in the field of Brain-Computer Interfaces (BCIs) due to the quickly growing nature of technology and research.

The information in this book is accurate, dependable, full, and suitable, but the author and publisher make no claims or guarantees of any kind, either stated or implied. Before making judgments or acting upon the information presented, readers are urged to speak with licensed professionals and authorities in the pertinent sectors.

The opinions and interpretations of the author regarding the current status of BCI technology and its implications are reflected in the content of this book. It is not meant to take the place of or serve as a substitute for expert opinion or professional judgment in fields like law, ethics, or medicine.

The use of or reliance on the information included in this book may not result in any direct, indirect, incidental, consequential, or punitive damages, under any circumstances, from the author or publisher. When implementing the principles and ideas offered, readers should use their own judgment and professional advice as necessary.

You recognize and agree to these terms and conditions by reading this book.

CHAPTER 1

EXPLAINING BRAIN-COMPUTER INTERFACES (BCIs)

1.1 The Fundamentals of How the Brain Works

It's crucial to first understand how the brain works in order to fully appreciate the complexities of Brain-Computer Interfaces (BCIs). The brain is an incredibly intricate organ that governs all bodily functions, including thought, memory, emotion, touch, motor skills, vision, respiration, and temperature regulation. Here is a summary of important things to think about:

Neurons and Synapses:
- There are roughly 86 billion neurons in the brain.
- The fundamental units of the neurological system are neurons.
- The connections between neurons, or synapses, are how they exchange messages.
- Chemicals called neurotransmitters are released at synapses to transfer messages from one neuron to

another.

Electrical Activity:

- Action potentials are electrical impulses that neurons use to communicate with one another.
- Brain electrical activity is measured by electroencephalography, or EEG.
- Distinct electrical activity patterns are produced by different brain areas and are linked to different cognitive and motor tasks.

Brain Regions and Functions:

- The brain is made up of the brainstem, cerebellum, and cerebrum, among other key regions.
- Higher order brain processes, such as motor control, perception of sensory information, and thought, are controlled by the cerebrum.
- Voluntary motions like posture, balance, and speech are coordinated by the cerebellum.
- Vital life processes including breathing, heartbeat, and blood pressure are managed by the brainstem.

1.2 A Technical Overview of How BCIs Operate

Systems known as brain-computer interfaces, or BCIs, enable direct brain-to-external device communication. Based on their functional principles and technical elements, BCIs can be divided into different categories. Here's a thorough rundown:

Signal Acquisition:

- Capturing brain signals is the first step in the BCI process. Numerous methods, including electrocorticography (ECoG), EEG, and intracortical recordings, can be used to do this.
- Electrodes are applied to the scalp during an EEG to measure electrical activity. It is popular and non-invasive.
- Electrodes must be positioned on the brain's surface in order to use ECoG. Although it offers higher resolution signals, it is more intrusive.
- The most risk-free method of recording, intracortical electrode implantation provides the highest signal resolution.

Signal Processing:

- Preprocessing, which includes filtering and artifact removal to improve signal quality, is necessary since acquired signals are frequently noisy.

- Next comes feature extraction, which identifies pertinent signal properties like amplitude, frequency, or particular brain patterns.

- These traits are translated into commands using feature translation, which can operate external devices.

Device Output:

- External devices like robotic limbs, computer cursors, or communication systems are operated by the translated commands.

- In order to provide efficient and adaptive control, feedback mechanisms are necessary to modify the BCI system in response to user input and device performance.

1.3 BCI Types: Hybrid, Non-Invasive, and Invasive

Based on the techniques employed to obtain brain signals,

BCIs can be categorized. Every variety has benefits and drawbacks.

Invasive Brain-Computer Interfaces:

- These BCIs entail the surgical installation of electrodes right into the brain. They deliver the best possible signals and can perform intricate jobs like delicate motor control of prosthetic limbs.
- They do, however, come with a number of serious hazards, such as tissue injury, infection, and long-term biocompatibility problems.

Non-Invasive BCIs:

- Non-invasive BCIs use external sensors, most frequently electroencephalography (EEG), to detect brain activity.
- Compared to invasive technologies, they offer poorer signal resolution, but they are safe and simple to use.
- Examples of applications are neurofeedback training, basic prosthesis controls, and basic communication devices.

Hybrid BCIs:

- Hybrid BCIs mix non-invasive and invasive methods to take advantage of their respective benefits.
- They seek to increase user comfort and reduce dangers while simultaneously improving signal quality.
- Though currently mostly at the experimental stage, these systems have potential for use in the future.

1.4 BCI History: From Idea to Implementation

Key turning points in the development of BCIs from a theoretical concept to an effective technology are as follows:

Initial Thoughts and Studies:

- The EEG, created by Hans Berger in the 1920s, showed that electrical activity in the brain could be monitored non-invasively and laid the groundwork for the concept of brain-computer interfaces (BCIs).
- The term "Brain-Computer Interface" was first used by Jacques Vidal in the 1970s, when he also carried out groundbreaking research that showed how to use

EEG signals to operate simple external devices.

Progress in the 1990s and 2000s:

- The 1990s and early 2000s saw a considerable improvement in BCI technology due to developments in processing power and signal processing methods.
- Among the notable accomplishments are the successful control of robotic equipment by neural signals and the development of dependable EEG-based communication systems for patients with severe movement limitations.

Recent Developments and Future Directions:

- Commercially available BCI products targeting the consumer and medical markets have been making an appearance in recent years.
- The creation of more advanced and minimally invasive neural interfaces, the use of machine learning techniques to improve signal processing, and the investigation of brain-computer interfaces (BCIs) for applications in virtual reality, gaming, and mental health are examples of innovations.

- Future directions for BCIs include enhancing their robustness and usability, broadening their applications across multiple disciplines, and combining them with other cutting-edge technologies like augmented reality and artificial intelligence.

CHAPTER 2

2.1 Restoring Motion: Brain-Computer Interfaces for Paralysis and Amputees

Brain-Computer Interfaces, or BCIs, have demonstrated enormous promise in helping people who are paralyzed or have lost a limb move again. By bridging the communication gap between the brain and external equipment, these interfaces enable mobility assistance and prosthetic limb control. The salient points are as follows:

BCIs for Paralysis:
- BCIs can help people who have spinal cord injuries or neurodegenerative illnesses like ALS.
- Brain-computer interfaces (BCIs) convert neural impulses linked to planned movements into commands for external devices.
- Examples include thinking your way into

manipulating a wheelchair or robotic arms.

- Studies have indicated that brain-computer interfaces (BCIs) can assist paralyzed people in executing tasks like manipulating computer cursors or gripping things.

Prosthetic Limbs for Amputees:

- Through the use of BCIs, amputees can manipulate prosthetic limbs in a way that closely resembles their normal range of motion.
- While myoelectric prosthetics rely on muscle signals, brain-computer interfaces (BCIs) use direct neural signals.
- This technology makes control more intuitive and precise, which enhances the user's capacity to carry out challenging activities.
- One advancement is the creation of prosthetics with several degrees of freedom, which enable fingers to move independently and offer more useful and adaptable options.

2.2 Managing Neurological Conditions: Depression, Parkinson's, and Epilepsy

Significant progress is being made in the treatment of several neurological illnesses with BCIs. These technologies provide new therapeutic options for illnesses that were previously difficult to successfully control by directly interacting with the brain.

Parkinson's Disease:

- One well-known BCI treatment for Parkinson's is deep brain stimulation (DBS).
- Electrical impulses are delivered by electrodes implanted in particular brain regions to modify neural activity.
- This can help with symptoms like bradykinesia, stiffness, and tremors (slowness of movement).
- Adaptive DBS system advancements improve treatment efficacy by allowing real-time adjustment of stimulation parameters based on the patient's neural activity.

Epilepsy:

- BCIs are useful in anticipating and averting epileptic seizures.
- Implanted gadgets track brain activity and identify precursors to seizures.
- When these devices identify abnormal neurological activity, they can interrupt it with electrical stimulation, which stops the seizure from happening.
- Long-term research has demonstrated promise in lowering seizure frequency and intensity in individuals with drug-resistant epilepsy.

Depression:

- BCIs give patients with treatment-resistant depression fresh hope.
- Methods such as DBS and transcranial magnetic stimulation (TMS) focus on certain brain areas linked to mood regulation.
- These techniques have demonstrated efficaciousness in mitigating depression symptoms by modulating brain pathways.
- Treatment regimens that are specifically tailored to each patient's neurological pattern using

brain-computer interfaces (BCIs) are being developed in order to achieve better results.

2.3 Improving Sensory Awareness: Artificial Hearing and Vision

In addition, BCIs are transforming the area of sensory prosthetics by opening up new possibilities for helping people who have lost their ability to perceive certain stimuli—such as vision or hearing—to regain or improve them.

Prosthetic Vision:
- The state-of-the-art advancements in this field include cortical visual prostheses and retinal implants.
- Microelectrode arrays are positioned on the retina via retinal implants such as the Argus II in order to activate the retina's surviving cells and send visual data to the brain.
- Cortical visual prostheses excite the visual cortex directly, avoiding the injured eye. These devices create a kind of artificial vision by using cameras to

take pictures and translating them into electrical signals that the brain can understand.

Prosthetic Hearing:

- The most popular type of auditory prostheses is cochlear implants.
- These gadgets stimulate the auditory nerve directly, avoiding damaged ear tissue.
- Together with an internal receiver and electrode array, they also include an external microphone and speech processor.
- Many people with profound hearing loss may now detect sound thanks to cochlear implants, greatly enhancing their quality of life.

2.4 Brain-Machine Interfaces in Rehabilitative and Surgical Settings

By improving accuracy, safety, and recovery results, BCIs are revolutionizing surgical operations and rehabilitation.

Surgical Applications:

- Intraoperative Brain-Computer Interfaces (BCIs)

give surgeons immediate feedback, increasing the precision of brain procedures.

- Critical brain regions are identified and preserved during tumor resections or epilepsy procedures with the aid of techniques such as cortical mapping.
- BCIs can help with DBS electrode placement as well, guaranteeing ideal targeting and reducing issues.

Rehabilitation:

- BCIs are incorporated into stroke and motor disability patients' rehabilitation regimens.
- Exoskeletons or robotic devices controlled by BCI and neurofeedback aid in the process of motor rehabilitation.
- BCIs allow patients to rehearse motions in a safe setting while offering real-time feedback and modifications.
- Research indicates that enhanced brain plasticity using BCI-based rehabilitation can result in better motor function and a quicker rate of recovery.

Brain-computer interfaces (BCIs) are paving the way for

novel approaches in the treatment of neurological conditions, mobility restoration, sensory perception, and improved surgical and rehabilitation results. The potential uses of BCIs in healthcare are growing as technology develops, offering a more precise and efficient management of neurological and sensory deficits in the future.

CHAPTER 3

COGNITIVE ENHANCEMENT AND BCIs

3.1 Increasing Intelligence: Enhancing Retention and Focus

Brain-Computer Interfaces (BCIs) hold great promise for improving cognitive abilities including memory and attention. This field of study focuses on using BCIs to maximize brain function, producing superior results in circumstances that are both personal and professional. Important details consist of:

Memory Enhancement:
- BCIs can be utilized to activate particular brain areas that are involved in the generation and retrieval of memories.
- Methods including transcranial direct current stimulation (tDCS) and transcranial magnetic stimulation (TMS) have demonstrated potential in improving memory consolidation.

- Targeted stimulation has been shown in studies to enhance long-term memory development and information recall.
- Applications include improving learning processes in healthy persons and helping those with memory difficulties.

Attention Enhancement:

- BCIs can also be used to improve focus and attention.
- Through neurofeedback training, people can learn to control their brain activity to stay more focused.
- Research has indicated that attention training based on brain-computer interface (BCI) can enhance performance on activities involving prolonged focus and alertness.
- This has effects on a number of areas, such as professional development, education, and military training.

3.2 Accelerated Learning: Improving Academic Outcomes

By streamlining learning procedures and tailoring educational experiences, BCIs have the potential to completely transform the educational landscape. More effective and efficient learning outcomes may result from the use of BCIs into educational settings. Important details consist of:

Personalized learning:

- BCIs have the ability to track a student's brain activity in real time, giving valuable information about their cognitive state. By using this data, educational materials may be customized to each student's needs, resulting in the best possible learning environment.
- For example, the system can change the degree of difficulty or offer more resources if a learner is having trouble understanding a concept.

Enhanced involvement:

- During educational activities, BCIs can support and improve student involvement.
- Teachers can see when pupils are losing focus and modify their teaching tactics based on real-time

feedback on their attention levels.

- BCIs can be used to build immersive and interactive learning environments, which will increase student engagement and effectiveness.

Accelerated Skill Acquisition:

- By maximizing brain plasticity, BCIs can hasten the learning of new skills.
- Methods like brain stimulation and neurofeedback can improve how quickly motor and cognitive abilities are learned.
- Applications span from sophisticated technical training to language acquisition, offering a competitive advantage across a number of industries.

3.3 Innovation and Creativity: Unlocking Human Potential

Enhancing creativity and innovation is one of the most promising applications of brain-computer interfaces (BCIs). Brain-Computer Interfaces (BCIs) enable people and organizations to achieve new heights of creativity and problem-solving skills by using the brain's creative processes. Important details consist of:

Stimulating Creative Thinking:

- BCIs can be utilized to activate brain areas linked to ideation and creative thought.
- Divergent thinking can be strengthened by methods like TMS and tDCS, which can result in the creation of original ideas.
- Studies reveal that activating the prefrontal cortex might enhance creativity and performance on creative tasks like ideation and artistic pursuits.

Improving Problem-Solving Skills:

- By boosting executive functions and cognitive flexibility, BCIs can help people become more adept at solving problems.
- Neurofeedback training can assist people in creating more effective approaches to solving challenging situations.
- More creative and efficient solutions result from improved cognitive control and less cognitive biases.

Collaborative Innovation:

- By synchronizing brain activity across team members, BCIs can promote collaborative creativity, which can improve teamwork and collective problem-solving.
- Collaborative research initiatives, design thinking seminars, and innovation labs are examples of applications.

3.4 The Boundaries of Enhancement: Moral and Social Consequences

Even though BCIs have a lot to offer in terms of improving cognitive function, it is important to think about the ethical and societal ramifications of these technologies. Important details consist of:

Equity and Access:

- If access to BCI technologies is restricted to specific populations, there is a chance that it will exacerbate already-existing inequities.
- Preventing the development of a cognitive divide requires ensuring equitable access to technology that

promotes cognition.

Privacy and Security:

- BCIs gather private brain data, which gives rise to data security and privacy issues.
- Strong security measures are required to prevent unwanted access and exploitation of a person's neurological information.

Ethical Boundaries:

- Careful thought must be given to the ethical ramifications of augmenting cognitive capacities beyond their inherent boundaries.
- It is necessary to address concerns of autonomy, consent, and the possibility of pressure or compulsion to improve cognitive ability.

Social Impact:

- Changes in workplace dynamics and educational institutions could result from the widespread usage of BCIs for cognitive enhancement.
- It is crucial to think about how new technologies may impact cultural norms and values and to make

sure that their development and application will benefit all of humanity.

Brain-computer interfaces (BCIs) have enormous potential to improve learning outcomes, stimulate creativity, and improve cognitive capacities. To guarantee that these technologies are used properly and fairly, it is crucial to address the ethical and social consequences of them. It will be essential to carefully weigh these issues as BCI research and development progress in order to maximize their potential and minimize any hazards.

CHAPTER 4

COMMUNICATION WITH BCIs

4.1 Shattering the Silence: BCIs for Patients Who Are Locked In

Patients with locked-in syndrome, a disease in which a person is completely cognizant but unable to move or communicate due to complete paralysis of nearly all voluntary muscles, can now benefit from innovative treatments thanks to brain-computer interfaces, or BCIs. Through the use of BCIs, patients are able to communicate directly with an external device from their brains and engage with the outside world.

Restoring Communication:

- BCIs convert brain signals into speech or text, allowing patients who are confined to communicate.
- These systems usually detect brain activity associated with particular intentions or thoughts using non-invasive techniques like

electroencephalography (EEG).

- These impulses are decoded by sophisticated algorithms, enabling patients to type words or phrases on a computer screen.
- Eye-tracking technology is frequently used in conjunction with BCIs to improve communication accuracy and speed.

Improvement in Quality of Life:

- BCIs give patients who are confined back their capacity to communicate, which greatly enhances their quality of life.
- By communicating their needs, sharing their ideas, and interacting with others, patients might lessen their feelings of loneliness and despair.
- BCIs also provide patients the ability to direct their surroundings with their thoughts, changing the lighting, TV, and temperature.

Technological Advancements:

- Research is continuously conducted to enhance the accuracy and speed of BCI communication systems.
- Advances in artificial intelligence and machine

learning are improving BCIs' capacity to interpret complicated brain signals.

- More advanced interfaces that enable the creation of natural speech and more user-friendly control systems could be among the upcoming improvements.

4.2 Mind-to-Mind Interaction as a New Form of Communication

Direct mind-to-mind communication is becoming more feasible because of BCIs, also known as "brain-to-brain interfaces" (BBIs). The study of the possibility of direct brain-to-brain transmission of ideas and data is an emerging field.

Principles of Mind-to-Mind Communication:
- BBIs entail taking neural signals from the brain of the sender, processing the data, and sending it to the brain of the recipient.
- These signals are interpreted by the receiver's brain, enabling information interchange without the use of written or spoken words.

- To convey the information to the recipient, non-invasive BCIs are usually used in conjunction with neurostimulation methods.

Applications and Potential:

- Direct idea transfer is one way that BBIs could transform communication for people with severe disabilities.
- Examples of applications include group projects that allow members to instantly exchange ideas and thoughts, improving creativity and coordination.
- Compared to conventional approaches, BBIs in education could promote the transfer of knowledge and skills more effectively.

Difficulties and Considerations:

- There are considerable ethical and technical obstacles to overcome before achieving precise and dependable mind-to-mind communication, which is still at the experimental stage.
- Protecting the privacy and security of thoughts that are communicated is important, as is avoiding abuse or compulsion.

- As technology advances, ethical standards and legal frameworks will be necessary to handle these issues.

4.3 Language and Interpretation: Brain-to-Text in Real-Time

Because they allow for real-time brain-to-text communication, BCIs have the potential to completely transform language and translation services. Language obstacles can be seamlessly overcome by this technology, which can also give people new avenues for self-expression.

Brain-to-Text Systems:

- BCIs are used by brain-to-text systems to convert neural signals into textual language.
- Typically, these systems use non-invasive EEG equipment to track brain activity related to writing or speaking.
- These impulses are decoded by sophisticated algorithms, which then produce text that may be spoken by a speech synthesizer or seen on a screen.

Real-Time Translation:

- By recording ideas in one language and translating them into another, BCIs can improve real-time translation services.
- This could make it possible for people who speak various languages to communicate instantly, negating the need for interpreters.
- Applications include travel, cross-cultural cooperation, and foreign business meetings.

Inclusion and Accessibility:

- Brain-to-text technology can help people who have trouble speaking by making communication easier for them.
- For people with physical constraints that prevent them from using typical input devices, it also offers an alternate mode of communication.
- BCIs encourage inclusion and equality in a range of social and professional contexts by improving communication accessibility.

4.4 Security and Privacy Issues with Brain-Based Communication

Concerns about privacy and security must be addressed when BCIs are incorporated more deeply into communication networks in order to safeguard people's neurological data and guarantee the moral application of these technologies.

Neural Data Privacy:

- The very sensitive and private neural data that BCIs record provides insights into a person's intentions, thoughts, and mental state.
- Strong encryption and safe data storage procedures are necessary to safeguard brain information. - Preventing unwanted access, misuse, or exploitation of this data is imperative.

Security Risks:

- Malicious actors may use BCIs to intercept or alter neural data through cyberattacks.
- Maintaining the integrity of brain-based communication depends on keeping BCIs safe from

hackers and making sure that channels of communication are secure.

- To reduce these dangers, sophisticated cybersecurity solutions specific to BCIs must be developed.

Ethical Considerations:

- Consent, autonomy, and the possibility of coercion are among the ethical issues that arise from the use of BCIs for communication.

- In order to guarantee that people have control over their neurological data and the usage of BCIs, certain rules and regulations are required.

- Concerns including data ownership, informed permission, and the responsible development and application of BCI technologies need to be covered by ethical frameworks.

Brain-computer interfaces (BCIs) are revolutionizing communication by improving real-time translation, providing new opportunities for those with severe disabilities, and facilitating direct mind-to-mind engagement. To guarantee their responsible use and to safeguard people's rights and autonomy, however, strong privacy, security, and ethical considerations must go hand in hand with the development and application of these technologies. As BCI technology develops further, it has the potential to open up more accessible and inclusive communication channels, promoting better comprehension and a sense of community in our increasingly linked world.

CHAPTER 5

BCIs in Gaming and Entertainment

5.1 Virtual reality and gaming as immersive experiences

The gaming and entertainment industries are undergoing a change because of Brain-Computer Interfaces (BCIs), which offer remarkably immersive experiences. By combining BCIs with virtual reality (VR) technology, users can engage with digital surroundings in ways that are more immersive and interactive, expanding the possibilities for user interaction.

Enhanced Immersion:
- Direct brain control over game elements is made possible by BCIs, which makes virtual environment interactions more instinctive and natural.
- A smooth and immersive gaming experience is offered by the ability for users to manipulate objects and characters with their thoughts.

- This degree of immersion can improve the user experience by adding realism and interest to the gameplay.

Personalized Gaming Experiences:

- Based on real-time feedback from a player's emotional and cognitive states, BCIs can modify the game environment to better meet the player's needs and preferences.
- This customization can involve changing the storyline, upping the difficulty, or customizing in-game tasks according to the player's present situation.
- Tailored gaming sessions can extend player engagement and boost user satisfaction.

Virtual Reality Integration:

- More engaging and immersive VR experiences are possible when BCIs and VR headsets are combined.
- With just their brain impulses, users may navigate virtual environments, interact with virtual objects, and do challenging tasks.
- Applications such as entertainment, therapy, and

training simulations can all benefit greatly from this integration.

5.2 Neurofeedback in Video Games: Brain Training

Gaming is incorporating neurofeedback, a method that teaches people to control their brain activity, to offer amusement and cognitive advantages. In this procedure, BCIs are essential because they offer real-time feedback on brain activity.

Cognitive Training:

- Neurofeedback-incorporated games can assist players in strengthening cognitive abilities like memory, concentration, and problem-solving techniques.
- Gamers may instantly see how their brains are working, which enables them to modify their mental approaches and perform better.
- People with learning problems, ADHD, or cognitive impairments may benefit most from this type of cognitive training.

Reduction of Stress and Anxiety:

- Neurofeedback games can be used to instruct players in the management of stress and anxiety.

- Players can enhance their emotional regulation and learn relaxation techniques by mastering the control of their brain activity.

- By using these games as therapeutic aids, mental health and wellbeing can be supported.

Performance Enhancement:

- Neurofeedback games can help athletes and professional gamers perform better.

- Neurofeedback training can enhance one's capacity for concentration, quick thinking, and making decisions.

- This can afford you a competitive advantage in high-stakes sports and gambling situations.

5.3 Social Engagement: Virtual Communities and Converged Memories

By facilitating new kinds of online communities and shared experiences, BCIs are revolutionizing social interaction in the gaming and entertainment industries. These innovations have the potential to improve how people interact, cooperate, and communicate in online spaces.

Shared Virtual Worlds:

- BCIs can help create virtual worlds where users can communicate with one another by sending brain signals to one another.
- These settings are conducive to group projects, get-togethers, and multiplayer gaming.
- Users' sense of presence and connection can be strengthened in shared virtual environments, which increases the significance of online interactions.

Enhanced Communication:

- By permitting direct brain-to-brain or brain-to-computer communication, BCIs can enhance communication within virtual communities.
- Users can collaborate and engage in social interactions more successfully by sharing thoughts, feelings, and intentions.
- This may result in more deep and interesting social

interactions, especially on online social networks and multiplayer video games.

Community Building:

- BCIs can facilitate the growth of online communities based on common interests and pastimes.
- These communities can offer social connections, resources, and assistance to people facing comparable obstacles or aspirations.
- deeper social networks and a deeper sense of belonging among users can result from improved community development.

5.4 BCIs' Effect on the Entertainment Sector

The development, delivery, and consumption of material are all becoming more feasible as a result of the entertainment industry's adoption of BCIs. The manner that entertainment is received and experienced is evolving as a result of these technologies.

Innovative Content development:

- BCIs provide new possibilities for personalized and

interactive content development.

- By utilizing BCIs, content producers may create immersive and compelling experiences that react to the viewer's brain activity.
- Personalized music experiences, interactive movies, and flexible narrative are a few examples of this.

New Distribution Models:

- BCIs are capable of supporting new distribution models that place an emphasis on interaction and user involvement.
- By integrating BCI elements, streaming services can provide users with personalized content recommendations that are tailored to their preferences and brain activity.
- This has the potential to improve the audience's experience and lengthen their stay on the platform.

Improving the Consumer Experience:

- By offering more interactive and captivating content, the application of BCIs in entertainment can improve the entire experience of the audience.
- Players have the ability to actively participate in the

entertainment experience by changing the gameplay, music, or plot in real time.

- Improved customer experiences can result in increased contentment and allegiance.

Market Growth and Opportunities:

- There are substantial prospects for market growth as a result of the BCIs' integration into the entertainment sector.

- Businesses can use BCI technology to create new goods and services that set them apart in the cutthroat entertainment market. - More funding for BCI R&D could result from this, spurring more advancements in the field.

Immersive experiences, neurofeedback-enabled cognitive training, improved social connections, and a revolution in content creation and dissemination are all made possible by BCIs, which are also overhauling the gaming and entertainment sectors. With further advancements, these technologies have the potential to provide users with more relevant, customized, and engaging entertainment experiences. To ensure the responsible development and application of BCIs in entertainment, it is imperative to tackle ethical and privacy concerns.

CHAPTER 6

USING BCIS AT WORK

6.1 Increasing Output: Brain-Based Performance Enhancement

The use of brain-computer interfaces, or BCIs, to maximize brain-based performance is becoming more and more common in the workplace to increase productivity. These technologies present fresh methods for enhancing productivity, concentration, and efficiency in general.

Cognitive Enhancement:
- BCIs are able to track and evaluate brain activity in order to deliver real-time feedback on cognitive states like mental workload, stress, and concentration.
- By making suggestions for breaks, modifying the difficulty of the activity, or offering mental exercises to enhance concentration and productivity, this input

can be utilized to optimize work environments.

- For instance, BCIs can assist in determining when a person is suffering from cognitive exhaustion and offer strategies to address it; this helps to avoid burnout and sustain productivity.

Performance Monitoring:

- BCIs make it possible to continuously track a worker's brain activity, which improves the accuracy of performance and engagement ratings.
- Employers can learn more about the ways in which various tasks affect productivity and cognitive performance by examining patterns in brain activity.
- By customizing employment duties and responsibilities to match individuals' cognitive strengths, employers can increase job satisfaction and productivity.

Personalized Work Environments:

- By modifying tools and workflows in accordance with each person's unique cognitive requirements and preferences, BCIs can assist in the creation of personalized work environments.

- For example, BCIs can match an employee's cognitive state to match the work difficulty or provide tailored support, improving the employee's capacity to execute tasks efficiently. A more fulfilling work environment and more productivity are two benefits of customisation.

6.2 New Work Paradigms for Human-Machine Collaboration

New paradigms of human-machine collaboration are being fostered by the integration of BCIs into the workplace, which is changing the way work is done and improving the synergy between automated systems and human workers.

Enhanced Interaction:

- By enabling direct brain control of computer systems and robotic devices, BCIs enable more natural interactions between people and technology. This makes it possible to manipulate complicated systems more precisely and effectively, such as using only thought to operate machinery, data analysis software, or virtual simulations.

- Improved engagement has the potential to boost productivity and shorten the time needed for new systems and technologies to get trained.

Collaborative Robots (Cobots):

- BCIs are being utilized to create cobots, or collaborative robots, which operate alongside human operators to increase safety and productivity across a range of industries.
- BCI-equipped cobots can react to brain signals, allowing for smooth synchronization of robotic and human movements.
- Precision in jobs like assembly, quality assurance, and handling hazardous materials can be enhanced by this cooperation.

Intuitive Interfaces:

- BCIs can provide more user-friendly interfaces to facilitate communication with intricate hardware and software systems.
- Brain signals allow users to operate and traverse apps, analyze data, and carry out commands, negating the need for conventional input devices like

keyboards and mouse.

- This can enhance user experience overall, decrease errors, and streamline procedures.

6.3 Business Opportunities and Challenges

Businesses face both opportunities and challenges from the use of BCIs in the workplace. Gaining the most out of this technology and ensuring its successful implementation require an understanding of these variables.

Difficulties:

- **Privacy Concerns:** Since using BCIs requires gathering and analyzing sensitive neurological data, there are privacy concerns regarding the handling, storage, and protection of this data.
- **Ethical Issues:** There are ethical issues that need to be addressed because there is a chance that BCI technology will be abused to track or manipulate the thoughts or mental states of employees.
- **Cost and Accessibility:** Putting BCI technology into practice can be costly; for certain firms, the expense of development, implementation, and maintenance

may be a deterrent.

- **Technical Limitations:** Because BCI technology is still developing, its usefulness in practical applications may be impacted by shortcomings in accuracy, dependability, and usability.

Opportunities:

Increased Efficiency: By automating repetitive jobs, improving cognitive performance, and promoting more productive human-machine collaboration, BCIs have the potential to dramatically increase workplace efficiency.

- **Improved Employee Well-Being:** BCIs can help to improve job satisfaction and employee well-being by offering tools for stress management, cognitive augmentation, and customized work settings.

- **Innovation and Competitive Advantage:** Businesses can establish themselves as innovators by implementing BCI technology early on, giving them a technological and productivity advantage.

- **Enhanced Training and Development:** BCIs can be utilized to design improved training curricula that adjust to each student's unique cognitive needs and learning preferences, enhancing performance and abilities.

6.4 The BCI-Driven Workforce of the Future

The development and application of BCI technology is going to have a big impact on the nature of work in the future. Workplaces and the workforce will change as a result of BCIs as they develop further.

Transforming Job duties:

- By enabling new types of automation and technological engagement, BCIs will redefine job duties and responsibilities.
- As a result of increased brain signal interaction between workers and robots and systems, new job functions and workflows will emerge.
- Routine and repetitive jobs will be handled by automation, while more strategic and cognitive work will be done.

Individualized Work Experiences:

- BCIs will customize activities, settings, and interactions to each worker's unique cognitive profile and preferences, resulting in highly individualized work experiences for the future workforce.

- By matching activities to employees' needs and strengths, customization will improve overall work performance, job happiness, and productivity.

Enhanced Collaboration:

- BCIs will make it possible for human workers and automated systems to collaborate more smoothly and successfully, creating a more integrated and productive work environment.
- AI-driven assistants, brain-controlled interfaces, and collaborative robots will combine to complete difficult jobs and projects more quickly and precisely.

Ethical and Social consequences:

- To ensure responsible and equitable use of the technology, it will be crucial to address ethical and social consequences as BCIs become more common in the workplace.
- To preserve justice and confidence in the workplace, concerns including data privacy, worker autonomy,

and the possibility of cognitive manipulation will need to be properly handled.

BCIs have the potential to completely transform the workplace by increasing output, encouraging novel kinds of human-machine interaction, and offering organizations both possibilities and difficulties. The future of work will be shaped by these technologies as they develop, creating more individualized, effective, and creative work environments. To fully utilize BCIs in the workplace, it will be imperative to address the related ethical and practical issues.

CHAPTER 7

ETHICAL ASPECTS IN THE DEVELOPMENT OF BCI

7.1 Data Security and Privacy: Safeguarding Brain Information

The creation and application of Brain-Computer Interfaces (BCIs) raise important questions about the security and privacy of data pertaining to the brain. To ensure the proper use of BCI technology, it is imperative to address these problems.

Sensitive Nature of Brain Data:
- The information regarding a person's mental states, thoughts, and cognitive processes that is gathered by BCIs is extremely private and sensitive.
- This data raises issues about misuse and illegal access because it might reveal personal information about an individual's goals, feelings, and even cognitive vulnerabilities.

Data Protection Measures:

- To prevent unauthorized access to brain data during transmission and storage, strong encryption mechanisms must be implemented.

- To ensure that only authorized people and organizations have access to data, access controls and authentication procedures should be set up.

- To handle new threats and weaknesses, security measures must be regularly audited and updated.

Data Ownership and Control:

- People ought to be able to access, edit, and remove their own brain data, as well as having unambiguous ownership and control over it.

- Consent mechanisms need to be put in place so that people may choose to opt out and are fully informed about how their data will be used.

- Users should be informed of transparent data rules and practices in order to foster confidence and guarantee responsibility.

7.2 Consent and Autonomy: Moral Decision-Making

Making ethical decisions in the development of BCIs include making sure that users retain their autonomy and give informed permission while using BCI technology.

Informed Consent:

- Before providing consent, users must be fully informed about the nature, uses, and possible risks of BCI technology.
- Consent forms should be simple, uncomplicated, and devoid of technical language to guarantee that people know what they are agreeing to.
- Users should have the chance to clarify any doubts they may have regarding the technology and its effects by asking questions throughout the consent process.

Autonomy Respect:

- Acknowledging people's right to make educated decisions about their involvement in BCI-related activities is part of upholding their autonomy.
- Users shouldn't be subjected to undue pressure or compulsion while deciding whether or not to adopt BCI technology.

- Measures should be taken to avoid taking advantage of or manipulating people's choices about using BCIs.

Ongoing Consent:

- Users should be able to evaluate and amend their consent options at any moment, as consent is a continuous process.
- To maintain continuing informed consent, users should receive regular updates and notices regarding changes in technology, data practices, or study findings.
- Users should be able to revoke their consent at any moment, and there should be explicit processes in place for deleting data and ending BCI use.

7.3 Fairness and Accessibility: Guaranteeing Equitable Benefits of BCI

To avoid inequities and guarantee that everyone can benefit from BCI technology, equality and accessibility in BCI development are crucial.

Addressing Disparities:

- Disparities in access to BCI technology should be addressed, taking into account variables including socioeconomic status, location, and disability.
- It is important to create programs and efforts that offer marginalized or underprivileged populations resources and support so they can take advantage of breakthroughs in BCI.

Affordability:

- It is important to take into account the expense of BCI technology in order to make sure that a broad spectrum of people can afford and utilize it.
- For individuals who cannot afford the technology, access may need to be supported by grants, subsidies, or financial assistance programs.
- Affordability issues can be addressed by cooperation between public and commercial sector entities as well as non-profit groups.

Inclusive Design:

- BCI technology should be created with inclusivity in mind, taking into account the requirements of a wide range of users, including those who are disabled.

- BCI applications and interfaces should be developed using user-centered design concepts to guarantee that they are accessible and useful by everyone.

- Diverse user groups' input should be taken into account during the design and testing stages in order to remove any obstacles and improve usability.

7.4 Long-Term Effects: Cultural and Societal Consequences

In order to mitigate potential negative effects and guarantee favorable results, the long-term effects of BCI technology on society and culture must be thoroughly examined.

Social Changes:

- The broad use of BCI technology could result in profound modifications to social dynamics, such as adjustments to how individuals interact, communicate, and work.

- Technology has the ability to improve human capacities, but if it is not managed properly, it could also result in new kinds of exclusion or inequality.

- The integration of BCIs may cause societal norms and values to change, requiring constant discussion and adjustment.

Cultural Impact:

- By changing how people see and express themselves, BCIs may have an impact on cultural customs and practices.
- The introduction of new forms of expression and interaction by technology could have an impact on creative fields, including art and entertainment.
- varied cultures and societies will have varied cultural views about BCIs, which will have an impact on how the technology is viewed and used.

Ethical and Moral Considerations:

- The possibility that BCIs will affect or control cognitive processes presents moral and ethical issues regarding free will and human autonomy.
- Concerns regarding cognitive augmentation, mind reading, and the possibility of BCI technology misuse require ongoing ethical conversations and

research.

- It will be essential to establish ethical frameworks and guidelines to direct the appropriate development and use of BCIs.

A variety of concerns are taken into account when developing BCIs, including privacy and data security, autonomy and permission, equity and accessibility, and long-term societal and cultural effects. It is crucial to take these factors into account in order to guarantee that BCI technology is created and applied in a way that upholds people's rights, encourages equity, and benefits society as a whole.

CHAPTER 8

BCIs' Social Impact

8.1 Transitional Connections: Social Dynamics in a BCI Environment

Brain-Computer Interfaces, or BCIs, are transforming social interactions and interpersonal relationships by posing new possibilities and difficulties for human connection and communication.

Enhanced Communication:
- By permitting direct brain-to-brain interaction, BCIs have the potential to completely transform communication. This can make it easier for more complex and rapid ideas to flow back and forth.
- BCIs, for instance, can help people with communication impairments express themselves more clearly and effectively, filling in gaps that more conventional means could not.

- Improved communication can result in a greater capacity for empathy and understanding among people, which may deepen interpersonal bonds.

Privacy and Intimacy:

- Privacy and the limits of intimacy are questions brought up by BCIs' capacity to access and share brain information.

- Maintaining personal privacy may grow more difficult if previously unthinkable methods of accessing one's own thoughts and feelings become available.

- It is essential to guarantee that BCIs respect people's privacy and set clear guidelines for information exchange in order to avoid abuse and maintain closeness.

Social customs and manners:

- The introduction of BCIs into daily life will probably lead to the development of new social mores and manners. People might have to learn new ways to engage and adapt to shifting perceptions and exchanges of information.

- The social acceptance of BCI technology and its ramifications will change over time, necessitating constant discussion and adjustment to preserve positive interpersonal relationships.

8.2 Learning and Education: Revolutionizing the Classroom

Because BCIs offer new tools and approaches for instruction and knowledge acquisition, they have the potential to revolutionize education and learning.

Individualized Learning:
- By tracking students' cognitive states and modifying the course material appropriately, BCIs can support individualized learning experiences.
- BCIs, for instance, can recognize when a pupil is having difficulty grasping a concept and offer customized assistance or other explanations to improve comprehension.
- By taking into account each student's unique needs and learning preferences, personalized learning can raise student engagement and results.

Enhanced Learning Experiences:

- By constructing immersive learning spaces, BCIs can improve student engagement and retention. Systems that combine augmented reality (AR) and virtual reality (VR) with BCIs can offer interactive, hands-on learning experiences.
- Students' educational experience can be enhanced by using simulations and real-time feedback to help them practice skills and apply knowledge in dynamic circumstances.

Monitoring and Assessment:

- BCIs provide fresh approaches to tracking and evaluating learners' emotional and cognitive reactions to educational activities.
- Teachers can gain insights into their pupils' development and areas in which they might require further guidance by using real-time data.
- Teachers can better understand and meet the different learning needs of their students by using this knowledge to inform their teaching practices.

8.3 Health and Wellness: Enhancing Life Quality

BCIs have the potential to significantly improve healthcare and people's quality of life by offering novel approaches to the detection, treatment, and management of a wide range of ailments.

Medical Diagnosis and Treatment:

- By tracking brain activity and spotting anomalous patterns, BCIs can help diagnose neurological and psychological disorders.
- By regulating neural activity and offering therapeutic stimulation, they can also be utilized to create customized treatment plans based on BCI data, which can improve patient outcomes and the efficacy of interventions for diseases like depression, Parkinson's disease, and epilepsy.

Rehabilitation and Therapy:

- By allowing patients to use brain signals to operate assistive equipment or take part in virtual rehabilitation programs, BCIs can help with rehabilitation and therapy.

- Patients who have had strokes, for instance, can use BCIs to operate robotic limbs or take part in cognitive exercises that encourage brain plasticity and healing. This method can offer more interesting and successful therapy alternatives while also hastening healing.

Mental Health Support:

- By recording brain activity linked to stress and emotion, BCIs can be utilized to monitor and treat mental health disorders.

- They can offer therapies and real-time feedback to assist people in managing the symptoms of depression, anxiety, and other mental health conditions.

- Personalized support and increased self-awareness are two ways that brain-computer interfaces (BCIs) can enhance mental health.

8.4 Law and Society: Emerging Frameworks for the Law and Ethics

As BCIs become more widely used, new ethical and legal

frameworks must be created in order to handle new issues and guarantee the technology is used responsibly.

Regulation and Standards:

- Standards and regulations pertaining to the development and application of BCI technology must be established by governments and regulatory agencies. Ensuring safety, efficacy, and ethical methods in study and application are part of this.

- To guarantee that BCIs are created and utilized ethically, regulatory frameworks should address concerns including data privacy, device certification, and clinical trials.

Legal Rights and Protections:

- Consent, privacy, and intellectual property rights are among the concerns that legal frameworks need to address in relation to who owns and controls brain data.

- Laws should define precise rules for data sharing, access, and utilization while safeguarding people's rights to their neurological information.

- Potential BCI technology misuse, such as illegal

monitoring or cognitive manipulation, should also be covered by legal safeguards.

Ethical Considerations:
- Concerns about autonomy, consent, and the possibility of cognitive augmentation or control should all be taken into account when developing ethical guidelines.
- Making sure that BCIs are utilized in ways that respect people's dignity and don't worsen already-existing inequities or introduce new forms of discrimination should be among the ethical considerations.
- Sustaining ethical dialogue and involving stakeholders will be crucial in tackling changing issues and encouraging conscientious BCI creation and application.

The social effects of brain-computer interfaces (BCIs) include adjustments to interpersonal relationships, adjustments to education, improvements to healthcare, and the requirement for new ethical and legal frameworks. It is imperative to take these factors into consideration in order to guarantee that BCI technology is created and used in ways that advance positive outcomes, uphold individual rights, and benefit society.

CHAPTER 9

PROSPECTS AND DIFFICULTIES FOR THE FUTURE OF BCIs

9.1 Technological Progress: Surmounting Existing Limitations

Although they are at the vanguard of technological advancement, brain-computer interfaces (BCIs) nevertheless confront a number of obstacles that must be overcome before their full promise can be realized. It is imperative that these obstacles be overcome in order to advance BCI technology.

Improving Signal Resolution:
- The accuracy and signal resolution of existing BCIs are limited, which may have an impact on their efficacy. Improving the accuracy of brain signal capture is crucial for more dependable functionality and correct interpretation.
- Improvements in signal processing methods and

sensor technology are required to lower noise interference and increase the precision of brain data.

Reducing Invasiveness:

- A lot of BCIs necessitate risky and complicated invasive procedures, such as directly implanting electrodes into the brain. Creating less invasive or non-invasive substitutes could improve accessibility and safety.
- Prospective fields for lowering the requirement for intrusive treatments while preserving good signal quality are wearable sensors and optogenetics.

Increasing Data Transfer and Bandwidth:

- The volume and speed of data transfer between the brain and external devices are impacted by the restricted bandwidth of current brain-machine interfaces (BCIs).
- For complicated interactions and real-time applications, higher data transfer rates are required. These constraints can be overcome by doing research on sophisticated data compression methods and high-bandwidth communication technologies.

Improving Long-Term Stability:

- In order to be practical for daily use, BCIs must show long-term stability and dependability. It is necessary to handle problems such as biological reaction to implants, wear and tear on devices, and signal deterioration.

- The longevity of BCI devices will be increased by the development of robust materials and technologies that are biocompatible and resistant to biological changes.

9.2 AI Integration: The Coupling of Mind and Machine

Artificial Intelligence (AI) and BCI integration has the potential to revolutionize both domains. This combination has the potential to improve BCIs' performance and expand the range of uses for them.

Improving Signal Interpretation with AI:

- By spotting patterns and correlations that more conventional techniques might overlook, AI systems might enhance the interpretation of brain signals. It is possible to train machine learning models to interpret complex brain input and produce results that are more accurate.

- Improvements in AI-driven neural decoding can result in better user experiences and more accurate device control.

Personalizing BCI Applications:

- Artificial intelligence (AI) can make personalized BCI applications possible by modifying systems to match the unique neural patterns and preferences of each user. Adapting interactions and feedback to individual users' cognitive and emotional states is possible thanks to machine learning algorithms.
- Customized BCIs can improve performance in areas including learning, mental health support, and rehabilitation.

Facilitating Real-Time Adaptation:

- AI can help BCI systems adapt in real-time by dynamically changing their responses in response to ongoing brain activity monitoring. Interactions become more natural and responsive as a result.

- Real-time AI-driven modifications can enhance BCI performance in intricate and dynamic situations.

AI Integration with Ethics:

- There are ethical questions about data protection, decision-making, and accountability when AI is integrated with BCIs. It is imperative to guarantee that AI algorithms are equitable, transparent, and compliant with moral principles.

- These issues will be addressed with the support of strong regulatory frameworks and ongoing research on moral AI practices.

9.3 International Cooperation: Establishing a BCI Ecosystem

Worldwide cooperation between academics, business executives, legislators, and other interested parties is necessary to create a full BCI ecosystem. Effective problem-solving and innovation can be fostered through collaborative efforts.

Encouraging International Research Partnerships:

- Research collaborations between institutions and nations help quicken the advancement of BCI technologies. Collaboration on resources, information, and skills can solve shared problems and result in breakthroughs.

- Collaborative projects and international research consortia can support interdisciplinary methods and incorporate various viewpoints.

Developing Standards and Best Practices:

- To guarantee quality, safety, and interoperability in BCI development and use, international standards and best practices must be established.

- Having uniform criteria can facilitate coordination and encourage creativity. A unified BCI ecosystem will be supported by the creation of standards for data formats, device compatibility, and ethical behavior.

Promoting Public-Private Partnerships:

- Partnerships between public entities and private businesses can propel BCI technologies into the marketplace and make it easier for them to be integrated into a range of industries.

- Funding, resources, and infrastructure required for commercializing and scaling up BCI discoveries can be obtained through public-private partnerships.

Encouraging Education and Workforce Development:

- Funding for educational and training initiatives is necessary to produce a trained labor force that will support the development of BCI. Governments, businesses, and academic institutions should collaborate to offer possibilities for appropriate education and careers.

- To prepare the future generation of BCI specialists, training programs should emphasize interdisciplinary abilities, such as neuroscience, engineering, and ethics.

9.4 Possible Hazards and Advantages: An Equitable View

Making wise choices about the advancement and application of BCI technology requires weighing the advantages and disadvantages of the technology. A well-rounded viewpoint can direct responsible invention and application.

Benefits of BCIs:

- **Medical Advancements:** BCIs have the potential to significantly advance medical treatments, such as the restoration of lost functions, the enhancement of mental health services, and the improvement of rehabilitation initiatives.

- **Enhanced Communication:** Brain-computer interfaces (BCIs) can open up new channels of communication and engagement, especially for people with disabilities. They can also speed up the sharing of information.

- **Educational and Cognitive Enhancement:** By offering individualized learning experiences and enhancing brain function, BCIs have the potential to revolutionize both education and cognitive enhancement.

Difficulties and Risks:

- **Privacy Concerns:** The gathering and application of

neural data give rise to privacy concerns, such as the possibility of sensitive data being misused or unauthorized access occurring.

- **Ethical and Social Implications:** Autonomy, consent, and the possibility of escalating inequality are just a few of the ethical and social issues that BCIs raise.

- **Technological Limitations:** To guarantee the sustainability of BCI applications, present technological constraints, such as problems with signal accuracy, invasiveness, and long-term stability, must be resolved.

Synergizing Innovation with Accountability:

- The quest of technological progress must be balanced with an awareness of the ethical, social, and regulatory ramifications. In order to minimize risks and maximize benefits, it is essential to engage stakeholders and implement responsible development practices.

- Constant communication between scientists, decision-makers, and the general public will guarantee that BCI technology is created and applied in ways that are consistent with societal interests and values.

Overcoming technological barriers, incorporating AI, encouraging international cooperation, and weighing advantages and disadvantages are all important for the future of BCIs. It will be essential to address these obstacles and possibilities if BCI technology is to advance and fulfill its transformative potential in a variety of fields.

CHAPTER 10

CONCLUDING THOUGHTS: AN EMERGING AGE OF HUMAN POTENTIAL

10.1 Key Findings Recapitulation

We go over the main conclusions from the investigation of Brain-Computer Interfaces (BCIs) and their effects in many fields in this chapter. A thorough grasp of the present and future orientations of BCI technology can be obtained by summarizing these ideas.

Technological Advancements in Brain-Computer Interface:

- BCIs have achieved notable progress in terms of signal resolution, invasiveness, and long-term stability. These developments are essential for the successful implementation of BCIs in real-world settings.
- Enhancing signal interpretation, personalizing apps, and enabling real-time adaptability are all potential

benefits of integrating AI with BCIs. It is anticipated that this synergy would spur other breakthroughs.

Medical Applications:

- BCIs have shown promise in treating neurological conditions like Parkinson's disease, epilepsy, and depression, improving sensory perception with prosthetic vision and hearing, and restoring movement for people who are paralyzed or have lost their legs.
- Novel approaches to enhance patient outcomes and recuperation times have been made possible by the application of BCIs in surgery and rehabilitation.

Cognitive Enhancement and Communication:

- Brain-computer interfaces (BCIs) hold promise for improving cognitive abilities like memory and attention, quickening the learning process, and opening up new avenues for creativity and innovation.
- For those with severe disabilities, brain-computer interfaces (BCIs) provide revolutionary opportunities in communication by facilitating

real-time brain-to-text translation and mind-to-mind contact.

Ethical and Social Considerations:

- Privacy and data security, autonomy and consent, equity and accessibility, and long-term social effects are only a few of the significant ethical issues raised by the development and application of BCIs.
- It is imperative that these issues are resolved to guarantee that BCI technology is applied appropriately and advantageously to all parties involved.

10.2 The Path Ahead: Priorities for Research and Development

Future research and development initiatives will influence the direction of BCI technology. It will be essential to concentrate on these areas in order to progress the field and deal with current issues.

Reducing Technological Limitations:

- Ongoing efforts are required to raise long-term

stability, lessen invasiveness, and improve signal resolution. It will be essential to conduct research on novel materials, sensor technologies, and data processing methods.

- The current restrictions will be partially overcome by investing in high-bandwidth communication technology and creative ways to reduce the biological response to implants.

Integrating AI and Machine Learning:

- Improving signal interpretation, personalization, and real-time adaptability will come from using AI and machine learning in BCI applications more widely. It is crucial to conduct research on cutting-edge algorithms and moral AI procedures.
- Researcher collaborations in AI and neuroscience can spur innovation and open up new avenues for BCI applications.

Ensuring Ethical and Responsible Development:

- Strong ethical standards and legal frameworks will guarantee the ethical development and application of BCI technology. This entails taking care of permission procedures, privacy issues, and fair access.

- Developing relationships with a range of stakeholders such as the public, legislators, and ethicists will aid in the creation of responsible development strategies.

Encouraging International Cooperation:

- Establishing an international BCI ecosystem via joint ventures, standardization initiatives, and public-private partnerships will spur innovation and tackle shared problems.
- Diverse viewpoints and areas of expertise will be incorporated into the research process if a collaborative approach is encouraged in the creation of BCI.

10.3 An Appeal for Conscientious BCI Development

It is crucial that we approach development with a feeling of responsibility and a dedication to ethical principles as we enter a new era of BCI technology. The following steps are essential for directing the BCIs' responsible evolution:

Adopting Ethical Standards:

- Data security, user privacy, and consent should be given top priority by researchers, developers, and legislators. Accountability procedures and transparent processes are crucial.

- Every phase of the creation of a BCI, from research and design to deployment and assessment, should incorporate ethical considerations.

Involving Diverse Stakeholders:

- By involving a wide range of stakeholders, such as patients, advocacy organizations, ethicists, and the general public, BCI technology will be able to address potential problems and answer a variety of demands.

- Stakeholder participation and open communication can foster trust and support for BCI advancements.

Encouraging Equity and Accessibility:

- Everybody should be able to utilize BCI technology, irrespective of their financial situation or place of residence. Reducing access gaps will encourage benefits that are equitable.

- Efforts to lower the cost of BCI technology and increase its accessibility in underprivileged areas will lead to a more inclusive society in the future.

Promoting Education and Public Awareness:

- Increasing public knowledge of BCI technology and its ramifications will aid in decision-making and help people weigh the advantages and disadvantages of various options. Outreach initiatives and educational initiatives can raise awareness and participation.

- Informed conversations and decision-making will be aided by the provision of clear and easily accessible information regarding advancements in BCI and their effects on society.

10.4 The Ultimate Possibility: Transcendence and Human Improvement

The capacity of BCI technology to expand human potential and overcome established constraints is its greatest asset. Investigating these options provides a picture of a future in which BCIs revolutionize human evolution.

Improving Mental and Motor Skills:

- Brain-computer interfaces (BCIs) can greatly improve mental abilities like learning, memory, and attention. They can also help people with disabilities receive rehabilitation and enhance their physical capabilities.

- New types of cognitive and physical enhancement will be possible with the continued development of BCI technology, which could result in significant improvements in human performance and wellbeing.

Overcoming Human constraints:

- By combining BCIs with cutting-edge technology like artificial intelligence and robots, people may be able to overcome their conventional physical and mental constraints. Novel forms of human-machine cooperation and interaction may result from this.

- By investigating the possibility of brain-based augmentations and upgrades, we can redefine what it means to be human and push the limits of human potential.

Implications for Ethics and Philosophy:

- The goal of using BCIs to improve human performance brings up significant moral and philosophical issues regarding identity, autonomy, and the essence of humanity. Navigating the future of human improvement will require answering these concerns.

- Making sure that developments in BCI technology are in line with societal values and goals will need careful consideration of the ethical implications of this technology.

In summary, the development of BCIs heralds a new age in human potential, one that promises tremendous progress and game-changing opportunities. We can fully utilize BCI technology and negotiate the obligations and exciting opportunities that lie ahead by tackling technological hurdles, integrating AI, maintaining ethical principles, and promoting global collaboration.

ABOUT THE AUTHOR

 Author and thought leader in the IT field Taylor Royce is well known. He has a two-decade career and is an expert at tech trend analysis and forecasting, which enables a wide audience to understand complicated concepts.

Royce's considerable involvement in the IT industry stemmed from his passion with technology, which he developed during his computer science studies. He has extensive knowledge of the industry because of his experience in both software development and strategic consulting.

Known for his research and lucidity, he has written multiple best-selling books and contributed to esteemed tech periodicals. Translations of Royce's books throughout the world demonstrate his impact.

Royce is a well-known authority on emerging technologies and their effects on society, frequently requested as a speaker at international conferences and as a guest on tech podcasts. He promotes the development of ethical technology, emphasizing problems like data privacy and the digital divide.

In addition, with a focus on sustainable industry growth, Royce mentors upcoming tech experts and supports IT education projects. Taylor Royce is well known for his ability to combine analytical thinking with technical know-how. He sees a time when technology will ethically benefit humanity.